How Much Is 100?

by David Bauer

STECK-VAUGHN
Harcourt Supplemental Publishers

www.steck-vaughn.com

How much is 100?
Is it a little or a lot?

Could you lift IOO pennies?

Could you lift 100 books?

You can fit 100 sunflower seeds in one pouch.
That may not seem like very many.

But 100 seeds can grow into 100 flowers.
That many flowers could fill a whole field!

A sea turtle can lay 100 eggs in one hole.
That many eggs don't take up much space.

But 100 baby sea turtles can hatch from 100 eggs.
That many turtles could cover a whole beach!

You can fit 100 crayons in a small box.
That may not seem like very many.

But 100 crayons could be used to color enough pictures to cover a whole wall!

How long do 100 minutes last?

In 100 minutes, you could watch a movie.

How long do 100 years last?

In 100 years, you could live a lifetime!

If you had 100 pennies, you would have one dollar.
That may not seem like very much money.

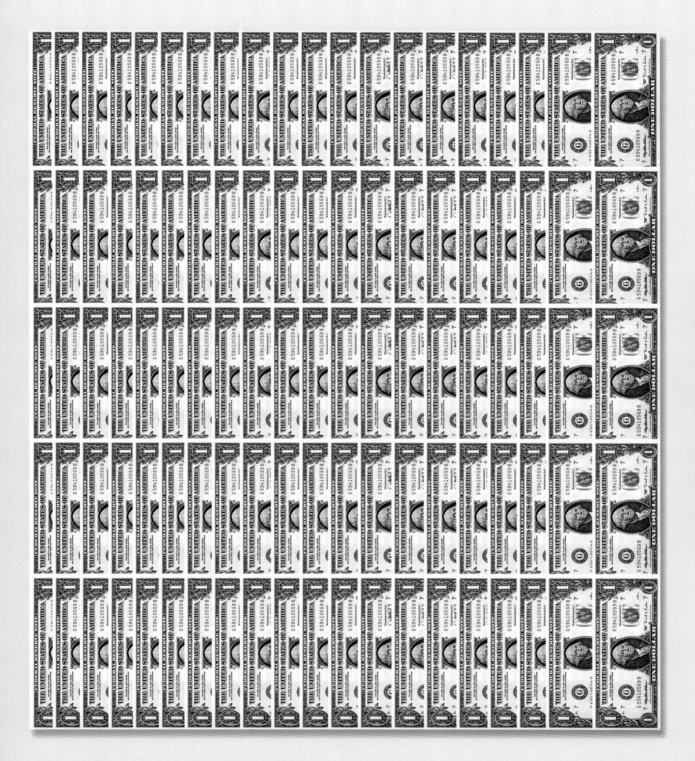

But if you had 100 dollars, you would have a lot of money!

You can hold 100 chocolate chips in your hands.
That may not seem like very many.

But 100 chocolate chip cookies are a lot of cookies!
That would be far too many for one person to eat.

With a little help, you could bake 100 cookies.
But that could take 100 minutes — or even more!